# CASSOCK IN THE KITCHEN

## *In the early days of women's ministry*

**Mary B Morrison**

ISBN-978-1-4716-0582-6

## Acknowledgements

I would not want to usher this little book into print without thanking a few people.

First, Rev Peter Neilson who in the midst of a busy life took time to write a kind foreword.

Secondly my daughter Flora who has given of her expertise, helping the manuscript to reach the publishing stage.

Many of those to whom I owe a debt of gratitude for helping me in larger or smaller ways are mentioned in the book and I can only repeat my thanks to those who have been most affected along the way because they were closest to me, Peter and our four children, Jane, Catriona, Sandy and Flora. After all, their "take" on it all might be different but that, as Flora says, is for their autobiographies!

## Foreword

If you know Mary Morrison, you will want to read this personal account of her life, faith and persistent calling to be a Minister of the Gospel. There is much to learn and lots of twists in the tale.

If you want a succinct summary of the social history of Scotland and the Kirk in the middle years of the 20th century, you will weave your way through social customs and educational systems that will bring back memories for some of us, and raise a quirky eyebrow for others.

If you need to be reminded of the jungle of prejudice and ecclesiastical hurdles facing women  following a persistent call from God, then you will be introduced to these barriers  gently and without rancour.

If you want to be a Barnabas-encourager to others facing difficult journeys with God, then come and meet a quiet group of travelling companions who saw the hand of God on this woman's life and helped her toward her true calling.

If you want evidence of the persistent, persevering presence of God in a person's life, you will watch threads being woven from childhood to adulthood, in education and Christian service, by inner conviction and external circumstance, until the will of God grows within and is mysteriously fulfilled in trust and obedience.

If you need to be reminded that ministry is rooted in a central core of the evangel with a constantly evolving shape of expression, then follow Mary from Townhill to San Antonio and travel with her from ministering amidst the tragedy of the Lockerbie disaster to being a chaplain to colleagues in the Presbytery of Edinburgh. The enthusiasm never wanes. The imagination never falters. The centrality of Christ is never lost

For five years, I had the privilege of working alongside Mary in the Team of Organisers for Evangelism. Her passion was always for the weakest and the places that seemed most hopeless. She believes in Resurrection as surely as her namesake in that Easter Garden.

Read on and you will hear the voice of the Risen Lord - perhaps stirring in you a dormant dream you thought impossible.

**Peter Neilson**

## Introduction

This is not a life-story - and yet it is! More accurately it is those parts of a life-story that reflect the progress towards fulfilment of a call from God to the ministry of the Church of Scotland. Of course many people experience that, but it happened to me at a time when that branch of the Reformed Christian Church was feeling its way slowly into new territory - the ordination of women to the Holy Ministry.

I first wrote some of this down in about 1988. At that time there were few women serving as ministers and it seemed a story worth telling. In 1992 I returned to full-time parish ministry after a spell with the Department of Mission and worked hard in that sphere up to retirement in 2000. Since then I have continued to fill in during vacancies and I took up a post as one of Edinburgh Presbytery's chaplains to ministers, caring pastorally for a number of those presently working in full-time service.

Perhaps my early experiences have become a curiosity as the years have gone by and people might be interested in reading, before it is forgotten, what it was like in the bygone days of women's struggle to be accepted more than forty years ago; the kind of issues that arose and remarks that were made when such an oddity as a woman who wanted to be a minister appeared, especially one married with four children! Indeed my declared intention caused one male cleric to immediately ask me, "Is your husband still alive?" The reader can work out his thought processes!

A woman in England where ordination of women at that time was even more unheard of than in Scotland asked, "Is Mary a man's name in Scotland?" Of the handful in Scotland who were already ordained when I began, most were single, one had two children and had been ordained in the United Reformed Church although she later ministered in the Church of Scotland, and not all were in parish work.

This is the story of how it all came about for me.

## Chapter One         Making It All Possible

I first heard it in the evening news broadcast. The sun was shining on a late May afternoon in the small village of Aberdour, where we lived on the north side of the Firth of Forth, in the Scottish county of Fife.

"The General Assembly of the Church of Scotland has approved a deliverance to open ordination to women on equal terms with men."

Always interested in church life and politics, I raised my eyebrows. I suppose in some ways it wasn't a surprise. Five years ago Mary Lusk, pioneering the field, had petitioned the General Assembly, our august governing body, to allow her to become a minister on equal terms with men. That petition the "fathers and brethren" had not granted.

But now in 1968 the permissive decree was passed in an imposing building at the top of the Mound in Edinburgh, from which you could see out over Princes Street Gardens and the New Town across the Forth to the North - indeed to Aberdour, where one young mother received the news with more than a little interest and maybe a passing nostalgia.

*Church of Scotland General Assembly Hall, Edinburgh*

This was the culmination of Mary Lusk's struggle. She was already a Deaconess licensed to preach but could not be ordained and so could not have her own charge or celebrate baptisms, marriages and communion (the Last Supper or Eucharist). She wrote of it in her book *Wrestling with the Church*. In September 2011 I attended her funeral service where Margaret Forrester, who had shared the early years with her, paid a moving tribute. There were others who felt called to be ministers but were not openly rebellious or terribly vociferous. It was hard to see why a Church that had a splendid record of sending brave women to the mission fields of Africa and India to preach the Gospel would not allow them to fulfil their calling at home.

The first breakthrough had come in 1966 with the decision to allow women to be elected and ordained as elders. In the Church of Scotland elders are lay people who assist the minister in the government of a local congregation. They share in pastoral caring and are likely to be involved in all aspects of church life. In all the courts of the Church (Kirk Session, Presbytery and General Assembly) they have equal representation with ordained ministers.

That decision, I suppose, must have registered with me but I do not remember. My first child, Christine Jane, was seventeen months old in May 1966 and I had just become aware of another pregnancy and was coping with being intensely sick and marking "O" grade exam papers in English.

For I was a qualified Secondary teacher of English, History and Religious Education, as it was then called. I had taught in Dalkeith High School until marriage to Peter, a lawyer and Procurator Fiscal, the Scottish term for a court prosecutor. In those far off days it was not unheard of for the woman to give up work on marriage if both were in a financially viable situation. As I write this I realise how much has changed socially in the last fifty years. I suppose it must have been about the end of that way of thinking - that a man should keep his wife! Certainly neither set of parents was surprised. It was the way they had known and as for my contemporaries it was still an open choice.

Thus it was that when the big decision was announced I was busy in the domestic routine in Aberdour, teaching in Sunday School in St Fillan's, the beautiful pre-Reformation church to which we belonged under the ministry of David Rutherford. How good to remember him and his lovely wife Jean and Jan their schoolgirl daughter. I attempted to keep my literary and intellectual awareness stimulated by marking the exam papers referred to and thus keeping a foot in the scholastic world.

*Family life in Aberdour*

There were lots of young mums at home in Aberdour. We met and shared baby-talk, and there were occasional chats over the fence with Mrs Levein who was bringing up her little boy Craig! It was a way of life that seemed likely to go on. So the news from the Assembly came and was absorbed with a mental wish of goodwill to women ministers of future days. Too late for me! If it had come just five years before I would have had a very different reaction. Then a door would have opened that had remained steadfastly shut, a door on which I had gently tapped.

## Chapter Two: 'The child is the father of the man' …. and mother of the woman?

*Four generations: with my mother, grandmother and great-grandmother*

"You hold the baby; now you are the mother and I'm the minister." Two little girls were playing indoors on a wet afternoon in 1942. One, the elder, had tied a large apron round her to act as a gown and now proceeded to climb up on an inbuilt window seat, overlooking a small neat garden with a low wall. Across the quiet roadway the Union Canal wound its way through this Edinburgh suburb of Craiglockhart to Glasgow. Often these banks were the play place, or perhaps the great green expanse of Harrison Park nearby, but today the girls were inside. The big Bible was now opened up and the baptism of dolls was about to begin.

This was a favourite entertainment. My little sister usually did what she was told and sometimes obediently answered to the name of Isaiah (an Old Testament book of the Bible!) What if there wasn't a father with the baptismal party? Most fathers like ours were away at the war anyway, fighting Adolf Hitler.

*With my little sister in Spylaw Park*

For the first nine years of my life this house in Edinburgh was home, from the day when I was brought from the nursing home at 5 Morningside Park. They were happy years, with Spylaw Park and Colinton and the Pentland Hills not far away. My father was a Pentland walker and from early years, to the horror of my mother on realising I had walked so far, I went with him "over the

Pentlands" accompanied by our Irish setter, June. Maybe it was these walks which gave me an abiding love of that range of hills and, in time, of the poet of the Pentlands, Robert Louis Stevenson.

Another walk my father and I used to have together was on Sunday mornings to church along the canal banks. Of course very few people had a car in the thirties and we walked most places, with the tram car desirable for a longer journey. There was always a point where we stopped by the canal and I was encouraged to say "Horsey, horsey" and hear the response of the animals moving and shaking their bridles inside the stables, presumably the Co-op stables between Merchiston and Viewforth. My father had a good imagination for children's entertainment.

The church we attended was St David's Viewforth, now long swallowed up by industrial premises. There were no creches in those days so my mother was at home with my baby sister except on the occasions when my grandmother came to baby-sit. And so it is that as far back as memory reaches there is church and the minister and God.

At that time the minister was Charles A. Smith, well known in Edinburgh because he was Presbytery Clerk. St David's had been the family church for many years and Mr Smith had buried my great grandmother, married my mother and father and baptised all of us, my brother joining my sister and me in 1942. So he was very much the family pastor with a round cheery ruddy face and a watch chain dangling on his black clerical garb. I remember him often in our home. His visits were regarded with awe but also with enjoyment. He was a friend.

After church  there was no tea in those days but aunts, uncles and cousins would gather for a "blether". For me there was Sunday School upstairs with little bespectacled  Miss Bell who must have introduced generations of children to *"Jesus loves me"* and to Jesus.

I always liked going to church. I was bored often, particularly with long prayers, but there was no embargo on stretching out on the red cushion-covered pew to sleep. Being the sort of person who can drop off easily, I had many a good nap in church!

We were taught to pray at home too, that Scottish favourite:

> *"This night when I lie down to sleep,*
> *I pray the Lord my soul to keep;*
> *If I should die before I wake*
> *I pray the Lord my soul to take.*
> *God bless........"* and then a string of names.

What a prayer for children! It must have had its origin in Victorian times when there was a large child mortality rate. Surely it is completely out of use now! However it didn't seem to cause us any apprehension and we went through the vain repetition quite unconcerned.

So as a product of Christian environment and nurture I did what we expect our baptised children to do, grow spiritually alongside physically. I do not remember a time when I was not aware of God within the limited apprehension of a child but there would come another influence that brought faith alive.

*And what would you like to be when you grow up?* - that question children hate. I don't know what I answered but from an early age I knew what the answer was. I wanted to be a minister, but I also knew I couldn't.

## Chapter Three: My Grandmother

She was one of the big influences on my life. Indeed, in accordance with the Scottish naming pattern I was called after her – Mary Brown. 'Gran' we called her, and she lived within walking distance. Indeed my mother walked every afternoon to visit her as I sat on the end of the pram that carried my sister. She was a widow, having lost her husband whom we never knew, not during the First World War but as a result of it. He was gassed at Ypres and really never completely recovered.

*With my grandmother in our garden*

With little social support in those days and being an active, intelligent person she ran a dairy in the "Southside", but that was before our time. When I knew her she had a nice Edinburgh flat with three boarders, a common way of augmenting income then. I loved going to stay with her and sleeping in the big brass bed. Later on she and my parents jointly bought a house in Blackhall, another phase which resulted in us all living together for about nine years.

But it is her sayings I remember most:

> *No royal road to learning …..*
> *Give to each flying moment something to keep in store …..*
> *If a thing's worth doing it's worth doing well …….*
> *Everything's mixed with mercies……*

I think she epitomised the strong Scottish qualities of her generation - hard work and thrift and trust in God. She and her sisters, all of whom we saw often, had been influenced by Moody and Sankey, and their trust in "Providence" was strong. Sometimes I would go with her to church in the evening to watch a lantern lecture, a kind of primitive slide show, frequently about missionary tales.

Eventually she had a terminal illness. I remember her quoting the hymn, *"I am trusting Thee Lord Jesus"*. I watched her die and among her last words were, "You'll not forget your Gran, Mary?" Indeed I haven't and her sayings still come unbidden to mind.

# Chapter Four: Schooldays

*This photograph of the three of us was taken to send to my father in Canada during the war.*

There are two great influences in the life of any child - home and school. Home I have described as modest but happy, leaving lots of good memories, and that is what I have always tried to build up with my own children and grandchildren - good memories. I remember the happy days in Harrison Park with my sister and the wartime concerts; the birth of my brother; the joys of reading. There was that seemingly wonderful woman Enid Blyton, who kept on producing more adventure stories, and there was an endless supply of school stories, and of course my favourites, the *Anne* books, all in the long dark wartime blackout nights in front of the coal fire. There were Friday nights with the release from homework, when my mother baked and we watched and licked bowls. Of course for so many of these years my father was missing, serving his country in the Air Force ground staff in Canada, but there were lots of great aunts whom we knew very well and who passed on their wisdom to us. They were my grandmother's sisters.

And school! I was privileged to be encouraged to have the education my mother could have benefited from but didn't have, and very much wanted for us. We went to one of Edinburgh's modest fee-paying schools. You didn't have to be wealthy to go to James Gillespie's High School of Jean Brodie fame (Muriel Spark was a pupil long before me, but years later autographed a book for me "from one Gillespie girl to another"), but you did have to be able to pass a test to get in and you were expected to want to do well academically when you did. I loved it!

There was a dedicated team of teachers, overwhelmingly spinster women, of the age group whom the slaughter of the First World War had deprived of potential husbands. They wanted us to use our minds and learn from what they shared of their knowledge. "*A man's reach should exceed his grasp or what's a heaven for?*" quoted Miss Andrew from her favourite poet, Robert Browning. She was our admired and distinguished headmistress.

JAMES GILLESPIE'S HIGH SCHOOL FOR GIRLS
STAFF 1955

*The staff of James Gillespie's High School*

Along with book learning went learning for life. Standards were high and those days were days of respect for authority, teachers, ministers, the nation's leaders and the royal family.

And God. Regular assemblies were held in the shape of religious services. The vast majority of girls would have had a church connection. Ideas in school were advanced enough for pupils to take part in the worship. A class would be responsible for providing a reader of the Bible passage.

I always had the reputation of being the best reader in the class despite being very nervous. On one occasion, aged 13, I was duly primed to read a particular passage to go with a hymn in the morning service. When the time came Miss Andrew announced a different hymn from the one we had expected so I, unauthorised, there and then on the platform decided to change to a reading that would suitably accompany "*God who made the earth.*" I proceeded to inflict on the assembly of patient girls the whole of the first chapter of Genesis about creation. Of course when we got upstairs to the classroom, an irate Miss Hardie demanded, "Whatever possessed you?" I duly explained that I changed the reading to go with the hymn. My gifts in arranging a service were not appreciated! Miss Hardie whom I idolised as an English and History teacher did not realise she had a future minister of the Kirk on her hands!

## Chapter Five: Still at School

Primary schooldays were dominated by the war, with air raid shelters on the Links, the open area we were privileged to have surrounding the school, gas masks having to be carried at all times, and mothers in charge of households. Queues developed everywhere especially when it was rumoured that a particular shop had a supply of a rare item. Mothers would tell others that an item of clothing like a winter "nap" coat was available somewhere and they would hurry off to get it. Rationing we were all used to but we were never denied parties. Mothers simply saved several weeks' rations to be able to bake and there were all sorts of substitutes like mock cream and parsnip butter. Eventually in 1945 the wonderful day of Germany's surrender came. It had seemed so near that on the previous Sunday Mr Smith had announced the timing of a service to take place when the cessation of hostilities was confirmed; so whatever celebrations may have been going on in London or even in Princes Street Gardens, my family were in church giving thanks! And there was much to be thankful for, not least that my father would be returning safe and well.

*With my parents and brother, 1948*

I always relate my first experience of answered prayer to wartime. My father crossed the Atlantic at the height of the Battle of the Atlantic in 1942 when the German submarines were active. I was old enough to sense how worried my mother was. I prayed and when we heard he had arrived in Canada safely, I believed my prayer had been heard. I have long believed that prayer is the secret weapon all Christians have available.

Slowly Britain emerged from war as we progressed at school towards the big leap into Secondary or the Higher Grade as it was then called. If I loved Primary I loved the new status even more. My interest lay in history, English literature and languages.

Of course there were opportunities to join societies. Among them was a branch of Scripture Union, or "S.U." as it was familiarly called. This worldwide organisation had as its core intention the promotion of Bible reading. There was a passage for every day and notes were supplied to enable understanding. The badge reflected the aim; the gold lamp on a green background and the motto "*Thy word is a lamp to my feet and a light to my path.*" Once a week in school there was a meeting of members for devotional purposes and in summer there were camps.

In Gillespie's the meeting was at 8.30 on Thursday morning for twenty minutes before school began. In Primary school I had become friendly with a girl called Joan Currie. Like me she came from a Christian home, in her case Baptist, and I think it was she who suggested we go along to S.U.. For the remainder of schooldays that was an integral part of our lives.

*At Gullane Beach with Joan, 1952*

Joan and I did lots of things out of school together, visiting the Museum on Saturday mornings and playing tennis in summer. We chatted and had teacher crushes as growing girls do, but we also always went to S.U.. Somewhere along the line, quite separately, we both committed our lives to Christ. In my case it was a natural outcome of years of worship and learning brought to a head in reading the Bible and having the evangel, the heart of the message, clearly explained. However much we are taught, we have to make our own individual decision about Christ, as in Jesus' own day on earth. For me it came quite simply, on my own, around my mid-teens. I always found it difficult later when some over ardent people seemed to expect a specific time and place of commitment. I'm sure that is so for some but it is wrong to suggest only a specific experience is valid. Christian growth produces Christians. Over and over again in the course of life I have made repeated commitments to the One I first learned to love as a little child.

For these reasons I support and encourage Scripture Union and the Scottish Bible Society. Much later, while minister in Townhill, I served on the Board of the then National Bible Society under the chairmanship of Fergus Macdonald. I believe in the converting power of the Word. Of course there must be teaching and we had that in the Saturday night rallies with Malcolm Ritchie and Heather Peebles -Brown, Ruth Samuel and Muriel Sayer, whom any of that vintage in S.U. will remember.

In time Joan and I along with Margaret Howieson became leaders of the Thursday meeting in school and served in various leadership capacities at camps. Not marrying, Joan continued as a camp leader for many years and must have pointed many in the Way. Four years ago she died of cancer and I was privileged to take the funeral service in her church of Wester Hailes Baptist and at the graveside at Mortonhall cemetery in Edinburgh.

For me this SU experience was all part of God's preparing me for ministry, though at the time that was still a long way off.

*The SU Group on Bruntsfield Links. Joan and I are in the centre of the front row.*

For the rest, school days and years went by filled with hard study, friendships, fun and laughter. My father came home again and in 1945 we moved along with my grandmother to a house my parents and she bought jointly in Blackhall, an upmarket but friendly suburb of Edinburgh where a whole new part of life was to open out. This meant the severing of ties with the old family church, St David's Viewforth, and the gradual incorporation into Blackhall St Columba's where we became a well-known family. Many new friends and opportunities awaited us. And for me it was another step to that fulfilment which was coming closer as the climate of thinking in the Church gradually changed. My own call was to become more insistent and I was to meet people who would give encouragement.

*Blackhall Church, Edinburgh*

The first minister we had in Blackhall was James G. Matheson who later became a Moderator of the General Assembly of the Church of Scotland, the highest office available and held only for a year. I was still quite young and he did not make an enormous impression on me. After five years he left for Knox Church, New Zealand. His successor R.J. Watson Mathewson is the Blackhall minister who stands out for me. I grew in faith with his two services each Sunday, as was usual then, and worked with him in Youth

Fellowship leadership. It was to him I eventually confided my desire to enter the ministry of the Church.

When he came to Blackhall I was in my last year at school and went along to his first New Communicants' class in 1952. This was a preparation class for what other branches of the church universal call confirmation. Vows are taken leading to full church membership and first communion. That particular Sunday is of course an impressive one. I was quite clear about my faith and I still have the Bible I was presented with on that October day.

A year later the end of very happy days at school came. It was June 1953, the Coronation month of a young queen in whom we, as slightly younger girls, had taken a close interest, and the music of our final school concert in the Usher Hall had an Empire theme. With all the necessary qualifications University beckoned, in particular the study of History with subsidiary English. Edinburgh was the only one of the ancient four seats of learning considered for application. The days of leaving home to go to University had not yet arrived if there was one in your home town.

It was of course a new chapter in life experience and a new step towards being equipped for the future which I saw as of necessity being teaching in Secondary School. I had inclinations in that direction and indeed it was my ability to teach and impart knowledge that later informed my preaching. But at the time it was a second best choice of profession for me.

# Chapter Six: University Years

Edinburgh University was the youngest of the original Universities of Scotland and had at that time only 5000 students, a small number compared with today. It was a privilege to go to University, not in the way that it was in England where wealth and social strata still counted, but because only about 2% of the population went and entry was entirely on merit with grants available. We were moving from the days of it being something unconsidered by working people with minimal education as in my grandparents' day, (although there had always been room for the "lad o' pairts"), through aspiration in my mother's generation to ours where higher education at school became more widely accepted and University was the natural progression.

Certainly it was the expected destination of all who took advantage of opportunities offered at Gillespie's and in 1953 I became the first of my family to matriculate at Edinburgh University. A good number of school contemporaries were there including my good friend Joan, although being on a different course we saw less of each other but met once a week for a lunch of pie and chips in a Drummond Street cafe.

That summer of 1953 my grandmother spent a long time in hospital and was sent home to die, though instructions were that she was not to know. So as I began University she declined and ultimately died on 25 October. I watched her lose hold on life sitting up overnight with my mother, sister and two of her sisters. It was a new human experience for me, one in which of course faith had to have play. Unlike nowadays, she died at home and lay till the funeral, coffined in our sitting room. She was buried in Seafield cemetery beside her husband and in the next grave is her favourite sister also with her husband. It was all grist to the mill of life, as we say, and she had left a huge influence on me.

University years passed successfully and happily and in some ways routinely. After a year I changed to make English my main subject and the next three years were spent in the joys of English language and particularly literature, loving Shakespeare and the poets and novelists. I have since attained a Bachelor of Divinity degree but literature is still my first academic love. Despite this, though, the two (in my opinion) outstanding lecturers we had were not actually in the English department. One was W. Croft Dickinson of Scottish History and the other was David Stalker of Biblical Studies who lectured mainly to postgraduates preparing for teaching; for after graduation came teacher training and the opportunity to study for Diplomas in Education and Religious Education.

Of course I met lots of new people. When you live at home to some extent University becomes a school add-on. Christian societies did not appeal. Joy Morrison, who years later would become my sister-in-law, was studying English two years ahead of me. I knew her from Blackhall Church. She encouraged Joan and me to go to meetings of the Evangelical Union. I went for a year but found it too rigid and gave up on the Christian side of University although there were two other groups in existence. Besides I had Blackhall Youth Fellowship and that was going to be a far greater influence on my future.

Having said that, it was midway through my university years that the famous evangelist Billy Graham came to Scotland as part of the "Tell Scotland" movement, which was a kind of national outreach organized by Tom Allan and D.P. Thomson, two distinguished ministers. There was an absolutely astounding response. People all over the land were talking about Christian things. They flocked to Glasgow's Kelvin Hall night by night. Busloads came from a distance. In preparation for his Edinburgh visit to Tynecastle stadium and for the relays of nightly meetings, counsellors were trained to help those who "came forward" as a sign of their commitment. My friend Joan and I were trained mainly by D.P. Thomson and played our part as the events took place.

As I said, the six weeks' Crusade was against the backdrop of "Tell Scotland", whose other method of outreach was visitation. Churches all across Scotland teamed up and sent people out in pairs according to the Biblical model. It was an outreach method I used later in my congregations with considerable results.

There is no doubt 1955 was a high point in church life in Scotland and the impact was felt for a long time. None of us then would have foreseen the position of Christianity now in 2012!

## Chapter Seven: The influence of Youth Fellowship

The Youth Fellowship movement began across Scotland after the war and made an enormous mark on congregational life. Young people in their teens and early twenties were encouraged to get together and with a background of worship and Bible Study to discuss the issues of the day as they influenced daily living. There was also an active social life and out of it all came not a few marriages. For many it gave opportunity to participate in leading worship and giving talks.

The Church was changing. Before the war it had been entirely minister-led; he dominated services and children stayed through them, going on to additional Sunday School and Bible Class, while there was no provision for older teenagers. In Blackhall the Youth Fellowship group was started by James G. Matheson who came as minister in 1945. He formed a group slightly older than I was, of able and committed young people, some of whom went on to a lifetime of service to the Church like Bruce Cannon and Stewart MacGregor. In addition to Sunday evening meetings, Mr Matheson took them to Iona of St Columba, and then of George Macleod who was one of Scotland's outstanding ministers. George Macleod founded the Iona Community. Its first priority was restoration of the ancient Abbey there. A community of eager Christians brought their skills and dedication, and when restoration was complete there grew around the abbey but also scattered across Scotland a community who saw their calling strangely enough as not monastic but as very much working out their faith in the world in politics and social awareness. They became a distinct entity in church life. Ministers were "members" and others were "associates" and there were rules about daily devotions and financial giving. Overwhelmingly the emphasis was socialist in politics and community. Many ministers who were Iona Community members intentionally served, often as their first charge, in some of the large housing estates and new towns that arose as Scotland struggled back after the war.

J.G. Matheson took his Youth Fellowship to Iona on holiday, and thus Blackhall young people were greatly influenced.

When I joined Y.F. I was not of the Iona mould nor did I ever embrace it, although I recognise the enormous contribution the Community has made to Scottish church life and perhaps especially to worship. The influences on my spiritual life were from Scripture Union where the emphasis was rather on the evangelical than the social gospel though I have long realised it is a mistake to separate these two. With the departure of Mr Matheson and the coming of Watson Mathewson, and the branching out in work and marriage of many of the original members, the strong Iona influence in Blackhall waned. Others came into Y.F. which remained one of the strongest in Edinburgh and I joined. This was to be one of the greatest parts of my preparation for ministry.

Watson Mathewson had more of an evangelical outlook though very theologically balanced and I grew to find in him a friend and mentor.

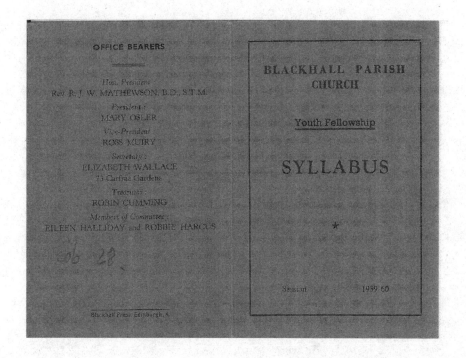

*Our Y.F. syllabus from 1959-60, when I was President*

Joy Morrison was studying English like me and we became very friendly, even meeting, just the two of us, for prayer in Blackhall vestry. I knew she had an older brother who occasionally appeared when home on leave from National Service but it was some time before I came to know him well. Joy and I went to Crail for a fortnight in two successive years with C.S.S.M. (Children's Special Service Mission), Scripture Union's outreach arm. Joy was two years ahead of me in study and so became a teacher before I did. She went to Glasgow and we saw less of each other for some years till other bonds united us. She married George Philip, a minister in Glasgow, and there they have remained.

I became Secretary and twice President of Blackhall Youth Fellowship, the majority of whom were students and graduates. In that post I succeeded Bruce Cannon who became well known throughout the Church as a Christian journalist and press officer. Of course all this was a massive lot of work but also tremendous experience in leading meetings and planning events. The Youth Fellowship as part of our Christian commitment took early Sunday morning worship in Ward 14 of the Royal Infirmary and in the evenings visited Ashbrook Home in Ferry Road. This meant the preparing and delivering of talks and prayers. Youth Fellowship members also went off together for a weekend once a year, first to old army huts at Longniddry and then to Dalmahoy. These times consisted of a mix of study and social enjoyment.

The weekend always ended with communion, necessitating the visit of our minister. When I was President we were gathered in the big room at Dalmahoy for the simple celebration to be conducted as though we were in the church building. And then my much-admired minister hit a problem! Normally the Y.F. President would act as elder and helper in the administration but could he allow me, as a woman, to do so? It did trouble him but he allowed it and I grew a tiny bit nearer ordination.

*Blackhall Y.F. at Dalmahoy*

Another experience that came my way as a result of Youth Fellowship involvement was an invitation to speak at the General Assembly's Youth Night. This was always held on Saturday evening in the days when there were no youth delegates to the Assembly. It was quite daunting to address a full Assembly Hall of all ages because, while mainly for young people, interested adults came as well. My topic was the Youth Fellowship movement. Ian Moir spoke on The Boys' Brigade. In later years I came to know Ian well as a colleague in ministry. Our reward for our efforts was an invitation to The Assembly Garden Party on Monday afternoon!

The ministry of women was being spoken of more and more, not least because the United Free Church of Scotland and the Congregational Church had already ordained them for some time.

Indeed two women I knew of, Betty Wardlaw and Jean Robson, had both left the church of their upbringing, aware of their call and impatient of delay. It was a course I knew was open to me - but not yet! I had completed teacher training and was starting the job itself.

# Chapter eight: Dalkeith High School

*With my class at Dalkeith High*

In the late 1950s Scottish education was being reorganised. In the state schools children came to the end of Primary stage and sat the "Qualy", the qualifying exam that sealed their fate for the next few years because as a result of that they went either to Senior Secondary or to Junior Secondary. In the former there would be a more academic education and opportunity to sit "Highers" in order to gain the Scottish Higher Leaving Certificate, whereas those attending Junior Secondaries finished at third year, the leaving age, and proceeded perhaps to an apprenticeship in a trade or other spheres requiring no academic qualifications.

But just before I began teaching, the Comprehensive idea had come in, with everyone progressing automatically to the same Secondary school, although within it there was grading of ability. Dalkeith High was one such - a new style of educating in a new building. I taught English, History and Religious Education up to Ordinary grade standard (a new fourth year exam), Higher certificate classes being reserved for more experienced teachers. I recall on a Wednesday afternoon having to teach half a class of boys while the others were out at games. You can imagine how they relished having RE on alternate weeks! What sticks in my mind is that, restless as they would often be as I tried to hold their attention, they became completely silent and attentive as we read the whole Gospel account of the trial and crucifixion of Jesus. The power of the narrative was self-evident.

I led, along with another teacher, the Scripture Union group and kept in touch after I left with some of the girls who were members. I also, along with the same colleague, ran the Drama club producing plays in the summer term. They were happy and fulfilling years with great colleagues and the usual crop of classroom problems. I have always said since that if I have had any success in my ministry it is because I know how to teach people, and it has certainly helped in the work I have done as a school chaplain. Teachers regard you differently if they know you too are experienced in their work.

But things were moving on. Still living at home as we did in those days and travelling on the no.18 bus, I frequently met Peter Morrison whom I had by now got to know in Blackhall Church. I found I had a lot in common with him and was vaguely attracted to him. To all intents and purposes it appeared life was relatively peaceful, but in fact there were problems and decisions being mulled over and prayed over in the background: and so I come to the next man who influenced the destination of my life, another male minister.

# Chapter Nine: Learning for the Future Still

"I'll teach you Hebrew and Greek, Mary."

I'm not quite sure how this came about but as already mentioned, before launching on the world of teaching children, there was naturally training - at Moray House College of Education. Alongside that I had studied for a Diploma in Education and a Diploma in Religious Education, both of which required attendance on postgraduate level at University. This was how I came to know David Stalker who had been minister of Aberdour before taking up his post of Biblical Studies lecturer in University. He was not part of New College Divinity faculty but part of the Arts world in the Old Quad. I found him one of the two best teachers I had in all the years of University study and of course I found the material fascinating. He was also someone intensely interested in his students and, as it turned out, a supporter of women in the ministry when it was still denied to them in the Church of Scotland. I came second in that class with a first class Merit Certificate and the outside examiner, F.F. Bruce a noted Oxford scholar, described me as "outstandingly good" in a letter to Mr Stalker after the exams, a letter I was allowed to keep.

More and more as I began teaching, the issue was rearing its head. I was feeling increasingly the call to ministry despite enjoying my work with the children. One summer evening David was filling in in an Edinburgh pulpit and my mother and sister came with me to hear him. From that there flowed a friendship that lasted some years and the offer to teach me the two ancient languages which at that time were required in Divinity studies. Of course I could have begun studying at New College, Edinburgh's Divinity Faculty. Women were admitted to study but not to ordination. In fact two distinguished women, Mary Lusk and Margaret Forrester, took that road, but I felt that till I was sure I could actually become an ordained minister there was no point in spending another three years in the ivory towers. Better to get into the world of working and earning. So it was a helpful step to be able to have language tuition from a scholar like David Stalker every Saturday morning.

He also pointed me in the direction of the London external Bachelor of Divinity degree and I enrolled for that. I was not his first protégée. Betty Kinniburgh was another woman with a ministry calling whom he had helped on the road. She too had studied at New College. All three of the women I have mentioned eventually became ordained ministers, as I did, all by different paths.

So it is that I owe an enormous amount to David Stalker, not simply for his teaching which was of great help when I did go to study full-time, but for his support and encouragement to follow what more and more I felt was my destiny.

The time came when it seemed right to share my thinking with my own minister Watson Mathewson. He of course had known me for years as I grew up and worked in the church and held office in the Youth Fellowship. But it was with a confidence that I entrusted him. I didn't feel yet that I could tell my parents the direction I thought I was moving in. They were happy enough with all my involvement in church life as indeed they themselves were similarly active, but for a woman to be a minister was still an aberration, a peculiarity. I had my career - in teaching - and one day I might get married - but a minister!!

Watson Mathewson listened and was cautious and vaguely supportive but I think he also thought it was a pretty big and unusual step to take. And of course, although it was talked of, it still wasn't a permitted calling in the Church of Scotland. Missionary work, yes, there were lots of them and they would come and speak, and on the great Foreign Missions night at the General Assembly (to which my father, an elder, first took me aged 13) they would be inspiringly dedicated. That was also a possibility. I used to tell myself that if I wasn't married by the age of thirty I would go to the mission field. Another option was the Diaconate. Deaconesses did good work helping ministers in parishes but were definitely number two in the job. As David Stalker said "You don't want to hang on to the coat-tails of any man." No, I wanted to do it myself. But though I didn't know it, it was still a long way off for me.

## Chapter Ten: Getting there … but not quite.

Thinking, praying, investigating and, courtesy of David Stalker, meeting women deeply involved in church work like Olive Wyon, Principal of St Colm's College, and Jean Robson who had herself become tired of waiting for the Church of Scotland and had taken the step of joining the Congregational Church, so it went on. I don't think I really doubted my own calling or that I could carry out the job, but was it wise to leave the worthwhile profession I was already engaged in and start on a long and difficult road? The way of pioneers is always hard. I was thankful for those who were so supportive but I equally knew that the idea was anathema and seen as unbiblical to many not least among the ordinary members of congregations.

But at last I took what at the time seemed a major step. I decided to train at the Scottish Congregational College in Edinburgh. Through David Stalker I had an interview with Principal Duthie who accepted me. I had all the academic qualifications required for entry but there was one requirement I didn't have. It was necessary to be a member of the Congregational Church for three years before starting training. Thus it was that on New Year's Day 1961 which was a Sunday, I was accepted onto the membership roll of Morningside Congregational Church, not too far from the school I had attended and in the part of Edinburgh in which I was born. It had been a sad departing from the denomination of my upbringing and the church folk I knew and loved. "You almost make me weep, Mary," said Watson Mathewson when I told him of my plans some time before. He included the following farewell notice in the Blackhall Supplement to *Life and Work* in October 1960:

*MISS MARY OSLER – It is with real regret on both sides that we say goodbye to Miss Mary Osler as a member of St Columba's and of the Presbyterian Church. For some time now she has felt the call to devote her life to the work of the ministry, but no opportunities to fulfil this call are, as yet – to my mind unfortunately – open in the Church of Scotland, so she has elected to join the Congregational Church, with a view to studying for the ministry of that Church. I would take this opportunity of thanking her for her many and much appreciated services to our congregation, particularly in the Fellowship and the Sunday School, and in your name of wishing her well in her chosen vocation.*

When it came to the bit my parents really raised no objections. I think they would still rather things were different but it was what I wanted to do and it was still a long way off.

In the meantime day by day all week I travelled out to Dalkeith and Peter Morrison, Joy's brother and member of Blackhall Church, was often on the eighteen bus on his way to his legal office!

## Chapter Eleven: A Change of Plans

Like many greater people before me I have never been clear why God works as He does but I am absolutely sure that when we have committed ourselves to Him, His hand is on our lives. It seemed now having made the big decision to join the Congregational Church and study for ministry in that denomination while my own Church wavered in uncertainty, that the way was reasonably clear ahead. Morningside Congregational became my regular place of worship and Philip Williams my minister, and with Sunday School teaching and gradual involvement and the occasional opportunity to preach, and my ongoing Saturday mornings studying the ancient Biblical languages with David Stalker, the path seemed set.

Within a few years I should be a woman minister, one of very few in Scotland.

But it was not to be. Peter and I had known each other for some time and had always got on well. We had long discussions together often outside Blackhall Church after the morning service. National Service over, he had resumed legal work at Balfour and Manson's in Edinburgh. There had always been I think an attraction. We were good friends to put it at its lowest. Then the day came when he invited me out for a meal. It happened to be the Saturday night before a Sunday when David Stalker, ever a great facilitator, had given me opportunity to take a service in St

Margaret's Juniper Green, where he was doing pulpit supply (i.e. filling in for someone on holiday). I had of course mentioned this to Peter over the meal but was astounded the next morning when I noticed him in the congregation at Juniper Green! As we saw more of each other the question of marriage arose. I had seen myself on one path, now another was opening up! I did not feel ready to accept a proposal at that stage. Indeed my mind was in a complete whirl!!

We knew each other, we liked each other but I believed I was called in the direction of ministry. We knew of quite a few broken engagements in our circle and I didn't want that. Just as I had had to be sure about ministry so I had to be more sure than I was about this. And what about ministry? As I've already suggested it was by no means general about 1960 for married women to have a career, and ministry seemed a particularly difficult one to combine with marriage and motherhood, because I would certainly want a few little ones about the house.

So after a few days of agonising I replied, refusing and indicating that it might be best if for a time we kept out of each other's way. This period he later referred to as the banishment! But there was always the eighteen bus where we passed the time of day as I travelled on my way to school.

To cut a long story short, presumably under God's plan for our lives, we were thrown together. One occasion was a visit to the Western Isles, North Uist to be precise, with my sister and my friend on holiday. The Morrisons' father hailed from there and Peter's uncle and aunt kindly entertained us.

In the same summer we travelled together to Ayr Kirk Week and spent a lot of time with each other in and out of the conference. There were three Kirk Weeks, based loosely on the German Kirchentag, with speakers and discussion groups. I had represented Blackhall at the first one in Aberdeen, where I was assigned a shared room with Nancy Paton from Dumfries, the niece of Scottish evangelist Tom Allan, minister of St George's Tron in Glasgow. I was thus introduced to him at the open air gathering in Pittodrie. Sadly he was lost to the church in Scotland through an early death. Nancy and I remained friends for many years, attending each other's weddings. When Ayr Kirk Week came along I represented Morningside Congregational Church, and discovered that Peter was also going. It was here that our romance progressed a long way and we agreed to announce our engagement at Christmas.

In 1963 as the leaves fell from the trees in autumn we were married in Blackhall St Columba's by Watson Mathewson. My ministerial aspirations were dying like the season. I had told all concerned that instead of working towards ministry I was getting married!

Norris
Edinburgh

I was welcomed back into the fold of my own denomination; my parents were probably relieved because it was more normal and a whole new future was dawning. Peter was now Depute Procurator Fiscal in Dunfermline and we had bought a house in Aberdour.

That is how when the General Assembly made the big decision I wished a blessing on those who would now be able to be ordained as women. I couldn't understand my situation - but I didn't try very hard. In the congregation at my wedding were David Stalker and Philip Williams, and Watson Mathewson was standing before us.

They had all been encouraging but all the hopes seemed at an end.

There followed six good years in Aberdour with Peter working in Dunfermline. Our first three children  Jane, Catriona and Sandy were born there and baptised in St Fillan's by David Rutherford, who is the first name in the visitors' book we have kept all our married lives, because he was our first visitor before we had handed in our "lines" or transfer certificates. I taught in Sunday School and Peter was ordained an elder. But as for ministry that idea was a "might have been" and I had no time to think about Hebrew or Greek and a London B.D. That was another life!

## Chapter Twelve: Another male promoter

In 1970 we moved because of Peter's work to Haddington. It was new territory to us, in the hinterland of Edinburgh in the beautiful county of East Lothian. With the removal van waved off, Jane the oldest and I went for a last time to the cafe in Aberdour. There was absolutely no way I could know how this move was going to influence all our lives! It was, after all, because of Peter we were moving. But in Haddington another man was awaiting me to be used by God. There were two churches; St Mary's where we felt the proposed restoration was perhaps not the wisest use of money, and the West Church, once the Free Church till the great union in 1929.

We eventually settled in the West where the minister was Joe Ritchie with his hospitable wife Frances, whom Peter remembered from University days, and their school age family. We were to come to know them all very well.

As we settled in and got to know people one sadness crossed our path, but death is part of life's experience. My mother died before the end of 1970. She had first been diagnosed with cancer five years before, recovering after treatment, but this time she did not regain consciousness following an operation. While we were entertaining friends from Dunfermline in our new home we were summoned by phone to go to the hospital. I had been very close to my mother and it was a sore loss, especially at the young age of fifty-eight. Still trying to keep my hand in academically, I was teaching evening class once a week and that helped enormously. With a young family there are constant demands and of course we had our church and our faith. For the Christian, death is never the end. The next year our third daughter and youngest child Flora was born, and that helped most of all.

Peter soon joined the West Church Kirk Session. I again took on Sunday School teaching, and as there was no organisation beyond that age for young people, the idea came to me on holiday during an evening service in the church in the Square in Oban, that I could lead a Youth group. By holding it in our house I could solve the problem of family bedtime. We had a large family house and a big sitting room. The indefatigable God was knocking again!

Working with the Haddington Youth Fellowship in the big room in Sidegate turned out to be among the most productive times of our life and it certainly brought revival to the West Church. We had happy, happy Sunday evenings, sometimes with speakers who always came to tea or stayed to supper. Sometimes it was Bible study on the syllabus. At that time some of the new, now quite familiar, songs were coming in; there were guitars and there was always fun and laughter. There were visits to big occasions, speakers like Nicky Cruz and gatherings of other young people, and there were weekends away to Yetholm and Kinghorn among others. Above all there was the joy of seeing young lives grow in grace and in favour with God and man. As I write I can still feel a warmth within as I recall the happiness of those years.

*In the Haddington garden with Joe Ritchie*

By this time it was permitted of course to have women elders but very few congregations had taken the step of ordaining any. Some women themselves were not happy with the idea. One evening we had a visit from Joe Ritchie, minister and friend. Before he left I had agreed to become the first woman elder in Haddington. Another had been asked so that there would be two of us, but being uncomfortable with it she had declined. The service for ordination of elders in the Church of Scotland is simple but meaningful and on a Sunday morning my service to the Church was in this way extended. I became a member of Kirk Session, the only woman among men but that was an experience I was to become used to.

I had a district and was able to exercise pastoral care of people. The *Haddington Courier* for weeks afterwards published a regular attack by a member of the "Church of God", a small group, on the West Church's ordination of a woman elder. Things were moving but I was still only doing what any good church member in the 1970s might do.

The more amazing thing was still to come; Joe Ritchie went on holiday and disregarding proper Church practice asked me if I would take the services for him!! As I absorbed the request I feebly said, "You know I once wanted to be a minister!" That was the first he had heard of it.

THE WEST PARISH KIRK

Minister: Rev. Joseph S. Ritchie M.B.E.,M.A.

OCTOBER NEWSLETTER 1973

West Manse
Haddington.
Tel. 2213.

My Dear Friends,

Our Winter season is getting under way and all our organisations are off to a good start. May God give us all good success in educating the young, upbuilding our youth, encouraging the adults, visiting the sick and befriending the aged and lonely. Though many problems arise to give us pause, the Christian life is essentially simple, following The Master and doing His Good Will.

A special occasion takes place on Sunday October 14th at the Ordination of Elders. This service is unique in that there is only one elder-elect and 'she' is to be our first woman elder. The Kirk Session decided to make approach to Mrs Mary Morrison, wife of our procurator fiscal to ask her if she would be willing to consider election to the office of the eldership. It was no light task to accept such a challenge but Mrs Morrison has agreed to be one of us in Kirk Session. We welcome her most cordially. As leader of our Bible Class and of our Senior Youth Group she is already deeply involved. She is well-equipped in many ways but none better than in her cheerful and friendly spirit.

Speaking of our Kirk Session - we have a wonderful potential in our present manpower and we should never lack for guidance and leadership. As a Presbyterian Church we are still very much dependent upon our 'Presbyters' or 'elders'. With each elder in his place at worship Sunday by Sunday what a witness and encouragement there would be to our own young people! And each elder engaged in some definite Christian service week by week - this is life and strength and joy to any congregation!

Next year we hope to be using our New Hymnary. What we have already heard gives us foretaste of good things to come. Different styles of hymnary, words, music etc will be on show in the vestibule for a few Sundays and orders may be handed to the Session Clerk. We hope every one will buy a copy. The West Kirk sings well and we do want to enjoy this new book of praise.

Remembering you all in our prayers,

Yours very sincerely,

Joseph S. Ritchie.

*The West Church newsletter announcing my ordination as an elder*

## Chapter Thirteen: Another Chance to Respond

It was ten years since I had been in a pulpit! The actual preparation was no problem. I did rather fear though, whether the congregation might wonder who this upstart member, really just one of them, thought she was; taking the minister's place. Going through my head as I waited in the vestry were the old words, words my grandmother had quoted in her last illness, *"I am trusting Thee, Lord Jesus, ......"* and the lines that say *"Words which Thou Thyself shalt give me, Must prevail. "*

The day wore on and as was still customary there was the evening service with a smaller number of people but with its own particular atmosphere. I have no idea what I said but I do remember that when I went home, on that June summer evening, I said to Peter who of course had been babysitting the children, "You know, I think I might have to think about it all again." It was a dreadful thought!

We were happily settled in a lovely house in a beautiful part of the country. Life was good. We had a growing happy family, three of them now at school. I was doing my bit in the church, elder, Youth Fellowship leader. Maybe one day when the children were older I would return to teaching. How could an upheaval like ministry - which was now of course since 1968 open to women, and there were a handful - how could that cut across such a happy existence?

*The children in Haddington days*

Peter listened and took it in his stride but there lay ahead a summer of indecision, what might have been long ago called "wrestling". We went on holiday to the North of Scotland, Contin to be more exact. Nearby was Strathconon and there Ellen Rutherford, deaconess and youth worker in Ross-shire, had established a centre for young people to come and stay. Ellen was the sister of our Aberdour minister, David Rutherford, and we took the opportunity to visit her and discuss my feelings and fears. Her particular comment which I have remembered over the years and used in sermons was this. "There is our time and there is God's time."

Of course Joe Ritchie now knew the whole story of my earlier progress towards ministry in the Congregational Church and he turned out also to be a supporter of women's calling.

But I felt I had one other escape route: Selection School as it was then called! All aspirants to ministry for the last few years had had to attend a selection process lasting three days with extensive interviews based on the Civil Service selection procedure. In the autumn I made application and attended a school just before Christmas in Glasgow. My mother's cousin kindly came to look after our children. But I was sure the powers that be would not accept me. How could a mother of four children ever be called to a charge, let alone study for a B.D. degree? And what about her husband? One elderly minister faced with this oddity said to me, "Is your husband still alive?"!

In early January 1975 it lay on the carpet - the letter I was afraid to open! I was accepted! It was a tribute to Jim Philip, Director of the School, that he had been able to lay aside his personal disapproval of women's ministry and recommend my acceptance. But any euphoria at success was soon replaced by all the implications. Peter, as his name suggests, has always been a rock. We moved into this together. The children were too young to realise all that it might mean. The congregation and most ordinary people simply regarded it as strange but, I suspect, probably thought I had something to offer. Joe Ritchie was thrilled. He had never had a Divinity student and he defied all criticism and all objections to my gender, because that was still a widespread attitude, by giving me countless opportunities to preach, assist at funerals and weddings and generally share with him in the work of ministry. I could not have had a more generous and helpful mentor. David Stalker, of whom I had seen much less after giving the whole thing up on marriage, and Watson Mathewson reacted with interest and pleasure. Said Watson, who seemed not too surprised, "God doesn't lead you so far along a road and then stop." He seemed to think the call was bound to come back.

God certainly hadn't let me alone and maybe as Ellen Rutherford said this was now His time.

## Chapter Fourteen: Preparation

Some wise person (and my life seems to have been full of them) once pointed out to me that Jesus was thirty before he launched on his ministry but all the earlier part of his life was preparation. God doesn't usually rush things and preparation is important. Of course much of what I had done prior to this was preparing me but now in October 1975 as I became a matriculated student once again, surely the final equipping was underway.

But still there were hurdles. In the late summer before term began my father suffered a major stroke and my brother, sister and I had to organize his long term care in hospital. He was thus not able to be part of the future significant events of my life, but I visited him in hospital on graduation day and he subsequently enjoyed happy hours in the Manse garden when we were able to have him out.

So College days began. Again I am grateful to so many people who helped with caring for Flora who was the only one not at school. Indeed because I had lectures to attend, she travelled with me and attended the University nursery for a year and during the next one she was sent to the Compass School, a prep school in Haddington. Because I had teaching training and a qualification in Scottish History, I was excused Church History and speech training and was able to attend lectures mainly in the morning.

*Faculty of Divinity, New College, 1975-6*

New College for me was a means to an end and I spent the minimum of time at the building. I did not need to socialise like young students and I had plenty of demands at home. Through lectures I got to know many who were afterwards colleagues in ministry but I didn't "hang about" at College.

My expectations of academic success were low. I who had never failed an exam thought I might have to get used to trailing along at the bottom of the class, but in fact that didn't happen. I think already being a graduate and knowing how to study, and having been trained at home and at school that "if a thing's worth doing it's worth doing well" (my grandmother again) all helped. In my first interview with Father Noel O'Donaghue my supervisor, I was duly asked about how I was going to manage as a student, wife and mother. He finished up saying, "Well you're not a perfectionist so you'll be alright"! At least he didn't ask me, as one of the assessors at Selection School had done, how I would cope if I had another child!

I was privileged to have Tom Torrance as Professor, though only for a term as he was nominated as Moderator that year. There was also his brother James with his lectures on the unconditional nature of grace. It was in New Testament studies however that I qualified with Honours under Hugh Anderson. I didn't find it too difficult to do well and indeed was awarded the Blackie Prize in New Testament Greek which required travel to Greece and Israel.

We decide to make this a holiday and took with us Jane our eldest, now 11, thinking she might remember. My sister and sister-in-law were good enough to care for the others for four weeks. Of course it was memorable though now it is fading after more than thirty years  but there will always be a thrill about walking where Jesus walked, lingering at the Garden Tomb and  I think especially at the Sea of Galilee, identifying in imagination with  another Mary the woman of Magdala, who found that Jesus really was a Redeemer. I have always particularly loved John's account of her realisation in the Easter Garden when the Lord pronounced her name that her loved Master was indeed alive. And of course there was Classical Greece!

All these experiences came out of New College where I spent three years. There was the simultaneous learning ministry in situ - in other words, the attachment. Two were required. The first I was allowed to do in the other Haddington church, St Mary's, where restoration was now complete and Jim Riach was minister. It wasn't a demanding two term assignment and it was here that I met the late Queen Mother who, staying with the Duchess of Hamilton at nearby Lennoxlove, came one Sunday to worship and we were all introduced to that gracious lady after playing our part in the service. Mine was to read the lesson.

*Meeting the Queen Mother at St Mary's*

The next attachment involved travelling into Edinburgh, to Mayfield in Newington where Bill McDonald was minister. Peter had known him at University when they were both doing a first degree. The important thing about Mayfield for me was that in the congregation in retirement was Professor James Stewart, a former New College teacher, a quiet gracious man, a writer of devotional and scholarly books and regarded as a saint of the church. Both he and Bill were supportive of women's ministry, because it has to be understood that despite the permissive nature of the Assembly's decision there were still many ministers and members antagonistic and disapproving. There were large numbers of congregations without women elders (now in 2012 there are still a few) and only a handful of women working in parishes. We were still a curiosity, and for some an aberration.

After graduation there was usually a probationary year of working full-time within one congregation as a trainee. Bill McDonald of Mayfield spoke for me to the appropriate committee in terms of my past experience, all I had done and still did with Joe Ritchie, and the upheaval that would result for the family if we had to relocate for a year. The committee granted me exemption. I repeat I have always had the utmost consideration and of course no-one like me had appeared before, so they were still working out how to apply the rules. This meant that in my last year at College I was free to be looking for a charge because I never envisaged anything but parish ministry. But this was to lead to the next agony.

## Chapter Fifteen: 1978

*With the family on graduation day*

Of course Peter and I knew when I embarked on ministry training it would lead almost certainly to a move. Now that it was coming I found it difficult to face. I had no doubt that his job had to continue. By this time he was working in Edinburgh, so I was certain I had a limited geographical choice. We had to be within travelling distance of the city. There was no shortage of ministers at that time. Some candidates were waiting quite a while before receiving a call to a charge. What chance had I with husband and children, especially when you subtract all those congregations who wouldn't look at a woman in the first place? As one lecturer said to the females, "You may have to wait a long time for a call. It doesn't mean there's anything wrong with you, it's just the way things are." There is no direction of ministers in the Church of Scotland.

And the children! For every mother these are her biggest concern. They were all happy at school and in the company of friends. How could I be responsible for tearing them away?

But it might be delayed yet a while!

Then there appeared a vacant charge in Dunfermline. We had been in West Fife before. It was reasonably easy to travel to Edinburgh so I applied. On a dreich day in March Joe Ritchie and I drove to look at Townhill. His sister lived just down the road and they had grown up in Dunfermline. Peter knew it from prosecuting in Dunfermline Sheriff Court. "We didn't get much crime from there" was his remark! I didn't find the place attractive. It had been a former mining village and had the stark council houses associated with such a place but the manse was nicely situated at the end of the village, reasonably private, and was an old Victorian house built in 1888. It was not as big as the Haddington house but adequate and attractive.

So it came about that in April 1978 on the Sunday after Easter a vacancy committee came from Townhill and the nearby village of

Kingseat to hear me conduct worship in Haddington and to interview me.

*Townhill Manse*

I can still hear the voice of our babysitter when Peter and I came home from a Kirk Session meeting the next evening. "You've to phone Mr Smith in Dunfermline." I did, and in the name of the committee he offered me the charge of Townhill with Kingseat. Of course I begged time to think about it. After a day or two I accepted and the children had to be told they were leaving!

But of course in that space my mentors had been consulted and had given advice. I had asked if I could meet with Professor Stewart whom I knew through Mayfield Church, and who had been appreciative of my work there. In his house that great man asked me to kneel with him as he sought advice and guidance for me. He said that because I was not drawn to Townhill as a place I would probably have a better ministry. I still have the communication he sent on my ordination evening.

So before I had sat my final exams, before graduation and licensing in July, I knew where my ministry was going to be. Among Jane's things I found a letter to her good friend Sarah saying, "I hope we'll meet again at University"- heartbreaking! In fact they didn't study at the same seat of learning but they are still to this day close friends. Of course we too had a lot to leave in Haddington. We had had eight good years, we left friends and a congregation. Time was when I had seen myself as succeeding Joe in the West Church because he would soon retire, and I thought that would be the ideal situation for us all. But I am told that kind of succession rarely happens. It was not to be. A year later he did retire and a new face came to the pulpit of the West Church.

Naturally there were several visits to the manse of Townhill before the flitting. One day some of the men of the congregation were working to put the garden in order for the new incumbent. I was introduced to them. One was Davy Bowden, an elder. Jane married Keith Bowden in September nine years later! But that is to run far ahead.

On a September evening a busload from Haddington and all our friends and relations joined the Presbytery of Dunfermline led by Douglas Aitken the Moderator, as I took the Church of Scotland's vows of ordination. Joe Ritchie and Bruce Cannon of Blackhall days spoke, Joe cleverly basing his talk on the reference at the end of Paul's letter to the Romans to "Mary who has worked hard among you"! David Stalker had to call off because of illness and Watson Mathewson already had advancing sclerosis.

I was the first woman minister in Dunfermline Presbytery as the papers pointed out. "I hope she'll be able to stand on her own feet" one male minister is reported to have said. They were afraid I would be looking for help from them! There were fewer than ten of us ordained by the Church of Scotland. Most were single and not all were parish ministers. None had four children to look after. I am still grateful to Townhill congregation who were prepared to take me on and give me a start.

"You won't get a dead congregation calling a woman," someone had said and so it proved to be.

It had been a long, long trail of winding but it was achieved at last with God's persistence.

## Chapter Sixteen: From then till now

It is now thirty-three years since I was ordained. They have been happy and completely fulfilling years. I have loved being a minister and I know there are some who have certainly benefited from my preaching and pastoral care. In Townhill our children grew up, and became a valued part of congregational life. Through the schools, Townhill Primary and Queen Anne Secondary, they formed their own friendships. Sandy's two best friends, one later best man at his wedding, were Townhill boys. Catriona came with me every week to the early service at Kingseat where she became proficient at the organ through the teaching of Bill Todd, an elder. I have a lovely memory of her playing and our family elder Jim Haxton singing *"Nearer My God To Thee"*.

Again we had a Youth Fellowship and took them off for weekends. An all-age group from the congregation had several weekends at St Ninian's, Crieff with Peter Bissett. What a loss there was to the Church's life when the decision was made to sell the Centre! As Convener of the St Ninian's Board of Management at the time, I spoke against it in the Assembly, but the course of withdrawal was set with St Colm's and Carberry also now gone as centres of education and relaxation for congregations.

In Dunfermline I was also appointed as Presbytery Youth Convener and was able to start regular youth events for the young of the area to come together. School chaplaincy was very productive and I was much welcomed by the headmaster John Wootton, himself an elder, who became a good friend.

We had some great worship. More and more, new music was coming into church life so there was new praise. Among the most memorable times were the Holy Week and Easter services. I had started these in Haddington and did the same in Townhill, meeting every evening to follow the steps of our Lord through that last week of his life on earth, and early on Easter Day gathering in the church garden to celebrate his rising again. For many people the whole event came alive in a way they had not experienced before.

Bringing my drama producing skills to use, I adapted and produced with members of the congregation the Easter parts of *The Man Born To Be King* by Dorothy L Sayers. Again this new approach spoke to people in a new way, especially those who took part.

A highlight of the ministry in Townhill was the celebration of 100 years of the congregation's existence, although not of the building because the people had first met in the iron church.

*Good years in Townhill*

We had many special events for the centenary, including a performance by the young people of *Joseph and the Amazing Technicolor Dreamcoat*, a service at which Bob Kernohan, then editor of *Life and Work*, was the speaker, and a dinner where the local headmaster John Wootton spoke. I produced *A Short History of Townhill Church 1883-1983*, and the elders presented me with the Mastermind bowl!

So faith was built up and from that congregation five ministers eventually emerged, among them my own daughter Catriona, making us the first mother and daughter parish ministers in the Church.

But that was still a considerable distance away. In the meantime Jane came to the end of school at Queen Anne High, distinguishing herself as dux and with several prizes and a place at Oxford to study German. By this time she was going out with Keith Bowden, who was of a Townhill family but now in his final year at St Andrews University. Eventually came the wedding earlier referred to, in Townhill Church with Joe Ritchie and myself officiating. If I had not gone there despite all the difficult decisions of that time in my career, they would not have met!

Throughout my time in Townhill I remained the only female minister in Dunfermline Presbytery, so I became very used to being alone in the company of varying numbers of men and to accepting comments of the population at large, at weddings and funerals. "We didn't know a woman could be a minister!" - implying that it was distinctly odd.

The local papers gave publicity to my arrival at Townhill as the first woman minister in the Presbytery, and then in the next May Mrs Thatcher became the first woman Prime Minister. As a result a little boy ran up to me in the playground with the question, "Are you the Prime Minister?" The church may have its problems but they are not as difficult as those of the nation. It was the same event in 1979 that caused Peter to say of Denis Thatcher, "There's another man who lives in his wife's tied house!"

In those days women had to decide what to wear. There is in fact in the Church of Scotland no prescriptive dress for men either but there is - or was - a customary one. Robes certainly add distinction and cover up any distractions there might be especially in a woman, avoiding the "What will she be wearing today?" We were anxious too as women not just to ape men but to be ourselves. I began by simply searching for high-necked blouses (one was acquired on a holiday in Paris) to go with a long black skirt. I had been given a Geneva gown, a Presbyterian preaching gown, at my ordination, and Haddington West had given me a BD hood at licensing, the ceremony that came on completion of studies. It was only later in my time in Townhill that I bought a cassock and could have been seen hanging out the washing wearing it in readiness for a funeral. With that came the "dog collar" which I now regularly wear. Dress as a whole with ministers, as in society, has become more informal but I still favour robes on Sunday and, like the Queen, respectful and appropriate dress at all times – but without the hat! I think many of today's women ministers dress in a very casual manner - but then so do the men!

At all times when I was working I have worn the Celtic Cross given to me by Joe Ritchie on my ordination. As people have admired it it has often become a useful talking point.

*The family on our last Sunday in Townhill Church, 1986*

My predecessors in Townhill, with the exception of the earliest one, had had only five year ministries. I stayed for eight. For the last few months I was looking around for something more demanding. It was a small place with great people but I felt in terms of building up a church I had given what I had. I think too I had enhanced the cause of women who were slowly increasing in numbers. One member of a congregation which became vacant soon after I left and subsequently chose a woman, said, "Because of you we chose a woman."

In 1986 I left Townhill, and was appointed by the National Mission Department of the Church as Regional Organiser for Evangelism. With Bill Shannon as Convener of the National Mission Committee money had been found to appoint five of us, all previously successful parish ministers (if there is such a thing) to cover Scotland, visiting and encouraging ministers and promoting ideas and methods of outreach by congregations. "Come over and help us," Bill said. Incidentally the other four were all men but it was never a problem. We were colleagues called and appointed to help and encourage our fellow ministers in developing missionary parishes. People in the church at large were beginning to see that it is not being male or female that counts but being able to fulfil the role. There are good and less good male ministers just as there are female. It is nothing to do with gender.

It was a very varied job, travelling in my case across the south of Scotland. I have visited most of the manses and enjoyed wonderful hospitality. I spoke at many Presbytery meetings and addressed Kirk Sessions, as well as writing materials for congregational outreach. Of course we met frequently as a group and learned much from each other. Peter Neilson was our leader, a man of great gifts and equally great commitment.

Out of this work came the opportunity too to represent the Mission of the Church in San Antonio Texas at the World Council of Churches' Mission Conference.

*Singing with the choir at the conference in San Antonio*

It was great to meet so many people from across the world and that is where I met Right Rev Lesslie Newbigin, Bishop of the

Church of South India and noted writer, who came for a few days and addressed us. John Bell also shone as Music Director, and I joined the choir. I produced the official English summary of the conference, *Acting in Faithfulness,* which was circulated widely. After the conference was over I was sent to preach at a designated church in Orlando, Florida, and then met up with Peter and Flora for a holiday.

This event led directly to my being invited to address and encourage the tiny Protestant Church of Spain in Barcelona just before Christmas. My kind host insisted on buying for me little painted statues of The Three Wise Men, Epiphany being the big celebration time in Spain, and they stand today on our mantelpiece.

I also represented the local mission of the Church of Scotland at a European gathering at Bad Herrenalb in south-west Germany just after the collapse of the Soviet Union, and heard amazing stories from delegates who had tried to keep Christianity alive in Eastern Europe. As I helped Hermann to produce our group's findings in colloquial English, he explained to me how he had learned a rather stilted English from books and had never been allowed to travel beyond the "iron curtain" to hear it spoken. Interesting and historic times!

Another experience that came my way through my position in the Borders was this. Everybody knows that just before Christmas 1988 a plane fell out of the sky and on to the little town of Lockerbie near Annan. Quite soon the relatives, mostly but not all American, were coming to see the place and identify their dead. All the ministers locally were involved in meeting them and sharing their stories of grief and I found myself too, travelling on Christmas Eve and during a few days after Christmas, down to Lockerbie and sharing in the listening ministry. I met Dr Swire who later became prominent among the bereaved families. At that time he was just a father who had lost a daughter Flora, full of promise. I too had a Flora, and we talked of Skye where his family had connections and which I know well. It was there that the remains of his Flora were eventually buried. There were others, and there was the moment of standing by the massive crater made by the bomb. Perhaps it was because it was Christmas that the words kept going through my head, "Emmanuel; God with us" because that of course is the essence of the Christmas message. We certainly needed God in Lockerbie! Owing to Christmas holidays the Scottish Bible Society premises were closed so I drew up my own list of what I considered helpful words of comfort, took them to the general shops where there was no difficulty in having them displayed, and they were very quickly snapped up. Cameron Gibson, the minister of Tundergarth where part of the plane eventually lay, asked me to preach at the memorial service there a year later. I was later invited to write about the whole experience in the Woman's Guild magazine, "Spotlight".

Another interesting thing occurred in these years. Although enjoying the work, I did miss leading regular Sunday worship with a congregation. During an apparently chance conversation with Bill Baird, minister of Inverkeithing St John's and North Queensferry, he invited me to assist him unofficially. This I did as and when available on Sundays for two and a half years. The service at North Queensferry came first, and among the congregation from time to time were Rev John and Mrs Brown, parents of Gordon, MP for Kirkcaldy and West Fife and later Prime Minister. One day there was a familiar yet not immediately recognized face. I was preaching, and as he left I asked if he had come to live in the village. He indicated he was staying with a friend. It was only afterwards, as we discussed him in the vestry, that we realized it was Tony Blair, at that time in Opposition. So on the first Sunday after he was elected in 1995 and became Prime Minister, I was able to say to the Stenhouse folk (where by that time I was ministering), "I'll only mention it once but I have preached to Tony Blair!"

Strangely, in the congregation at St John's Inverkeithing was a certain Rosemary Smith, who now says that I encouraged her early thoughts of ministry at that time. Last year I attended her induction to Townhill! Such are the ways of God.

We were employed for five years by the Department of National Mission and then four of us went back to Parish ministry and Peter Neilson went to a Mission Department post in "121", the Church of Scotland offices. He is now working freelance with congregations as a Mission Consultant.

Some people I think wondered what we had achieved in our five years. The jobs were continued though under another title. I think we did manage to heighten the profile of mission as the Church's imperative and to encourage individual ministers and congregations to engage with their parishes and communities. It is twenty years since I was doing that work but within the last month I was told by an elder whom I did not remember that my coming to his congregation had been "pivotal". I have reason to think there are others.

It was not particularly easy to find a parish at the end of a five year job. Whether people were suspicious of the fact that I had been employed by "121" or there was still prejudice against a woman, I was eventually called to a Lanarkshire triple linking, a country parish. It was not really my kind of place as a city girl and it had three services and three Kirk Sessions. The people were as kindly and appreciative as in any other congregation but I did not belong. I consulted several ministerial friends who said I should just move and it was with some trepidation I told the Kirk Sessions in slightly less than two years that I was leaving for Edinburgh. It was not really a very happy departure but I had done what I could while I was there and felt it was right to move. Our first granddaughter was born just before we left. That was the only time in my life I ever cancelled a Kirk Session meeting, so that we could go and see her for the first time. When I was inducted to Stenhouse St Aidan's in Edinburgh she was there, aged just three weeks.

*The Kirk Session of Stenhouse St Aidan's in our garden*

The years in Stenhouse were happy and fruitful. We started work among the young and built up a Wednesday club for school age children, a Monday club for young people and a thriving Mother and Toddler group which was the way of entry to church attendance and membership for some. A Young Mothers' group got going and a special meeting for older people which grew out of what was originally a Bereavement group. Eventually, as Sunday employment became more and more usual, we held a Wednesday evening service for those who could not attend worship on Sundays. Needless to say the congregation grew.

*Joining in with the youth club at Stenhouse*

Ministers so much need to be imaginative and inventive and as far as possible to make attendance at church easy for people in a completely different social setting from even fifty years ago.

One particular feature of ministry at Stenhouse St Aidan's was the challenge of being the first minister of a new union, a very unwelcome one as far as the participating congregations were concerned. For some years they had been linked; but had never worked closely. They had had frequent mentions at Presbytery for various problems. As someone put it to me, "Presbytery has put together two congregations who really don't like each other."

Someone else, on hearing I was going there, commented "Do you know what you're going into?" There were initial difficulties mainly because of entrenched positions taken up by organisations that wanted to remain independent of each other whereas I insisted we must be one congregation. A tribute paid when I left went as follows:

STENHOUSE ST AIDAN'S
Parish Church
10th. Sept. 2000

It is with grateful thanks that we, the members of this congregation, acknowledge the leadership of the Rev Mary B. Morrison, who by hard work and dedication to her calling, has moulded us into one cohesive forward looking membership prepared to undertake God's work.
We wish Mary and Peter a long and happy retirement and assure them of our thoughts and prayers in the years ahead.

School chaplaincy has always been an important part of my work. As a former teacher school was a familiar setting and I was privileged to teach in the classrooms as well as lead Assemblies. I never met any opposition and got to know the teachers well too. When I left, the children gave me what was so much better than any gift however valuable - a book of thanks for things they remembered and valued that I had taught them!

*Stenhouse Primary*

Ministers who regard themselves as too busy for school work are making a great mistake. That is where the children are and if there is one thing that marks the decline of Christianity it is that the church and Christian parents have not passed on the faith once delivered to the saints. In school we get the chance to present

what we believe and to explain the
festivals without proselytising but we
know that our God has his own way of
creating faith where the Word is
faithfully spoken.

It was from Stenhouse St Aidan's that I
retired. As it happened my sixty-fifth
birthday fell on a Sunday and I took my
last service followed by lunch in the hall on that day. I had
celebrated the millennium with that congregation and round the
hall Jim Brennan, our sign writer, had inscribed the names of
members at that time. I was sad to go but since I had arranged the
appointment of a deacon/youth worker I hoped all that had begun
might be continued.

*'Happy retirement Mary Morrison'*

*My retirement Sunday*

The family, having been invited with their musical instruments to take part in the service, shared in the lunch and then came to share my birthday in the new home in Inverleith in which we would live for retirement. They had prepared their own tribute to my ministry and retirement, to the tune of my old school hymn *Jerusalem:*

*And did those feet in ancient times*

*Walk by John Knox's statue tall*

*From there to parish work night and day*

*Waiting for Scotmid's funeral call*

*Or driving back from Galloway*

*Long committee meetings too*

*But now the bell of freedom sounds*

*So choose what you would like to do!*

*Bring me my spade to plant some flowers*

*Bring me my tickets for the play*

*Bring me my ladle to entertain*

*And let's both go on holiday.*

*I will not cease to work and pray*

*But only when there's time at hand*

*And all the family will gather here*

*In Eildon's green and pleasant land.*

After they left with their children - because the last ministry had seen the arrival of a few more grandchildren - we went out for a meal to Haddington, as I felt the need to fill in the day and wind down gradually. The next day was another new beginning.

But before leaving Stenhouse St Aidan's there is one outstanding event I must record. On a lovely summer evening in August

Catriona, my second daughter, was ordained by the Presbytery of Edinburgh in "my" church building.

Peter as a lawyer had had to make the case for her ordination to take place there, since the normal practice in the Church of Scotland was to be ordained to a position, most usually a charge. In fact she was going to minister in Germany where Marc, whom she married three days later, was a theology graduate. They had met at Tübingen University with whom New College Edinburgh had an exchange arrangement. Like me she had studied in Edinburgh, first German and then Divinity, and had been accepted by Selection School as a candidate for the ministry. In addition she had spent a year working for the Church of Scotland World Exchange in Pakistan in a girls' school in Lahore.

For generations sons had followed fathers into the ministry in Scotland, but we were the first mother and daughter. In March 2001 six months after my retirement I was invited by the Presbytery of Kirkcaldy to preach at her induction to the charge of Kirkcaldy Linktown with Auchtertool. They had come back to settle in Scotland and some years later Marc too became a minister of the Church of Scotland. This meant that with their growing family of three boys they could job share and in effect both work part-time.

Among our children and their spouses we have four elders and two ministers - a lot to be thankful for!

But how things have changed! On that night of Catriona's ordination I could not but think of the difficulties I and those just before me had faced in becoming accepted within the Church as women in the ministry. Those who think the Church never changes are completely wrong. The Church has changed enormously in fifty years, not least in ordaining women.

There are still those particularly on the Biblically conservative wing of the Church who would admit to not being totally happy at this change but many of such a way of thinking do acknowledge the gifts women have brought to ministry and what is much more important, there is no doubt of the help these women have been to those to whom they have been called to minister. I doubt if many women care about high office or wish to devote too much of their time to committees and administration, although we are all bound to give some. If I had not left Dunfermline when I did I would have been the first female Presbytery Moderator in Scotland. I did become the first female to be a Director of Selection Schools. Now women fill such a post in Presbytery as often as men.

There have been only two women Moderators of the General Assembly, one an elder. The one who is an ordained minister was not by then in a parish and has now worked for many years in "121". The number of ordained women is still small in comparison with men but it is no longer seen by society as a man's job!

We have come a long way.

# Chapter Seventeen: Retirement

*Outside Blackhall Church on our Ruby Wedding Anniversary*

Through all the vicissitudes of my ministry Peter, as his name suggests, has been a solid rock. Having been ordained an elder in Aberdour he went on to serve on all my Kirk Sessions. It was never a problem. As a lawyer he is by nature cautious but often also wise, seeing things from different points of view. I think he came to be respected by the other elders and as he put it to "find his place". He had been retired for some time and now I found myself in the same position. It was lovely to live in our own house. I did enjoy that and soon found that really ministers who are in health never need to be without work. In the Church there are long gaps called vacancies between one minister leaving and another being called. I was soon asked to do "pulpit supply" for ministers on holiday, and after we had joined as our place of worship the Old Kirk at Pilton, it became vacant and I was employed as locum there for two years.

Another vacancy quite soon cropped up at St David's Broomhouse and I spent a happy spell there being locum and Interim Moderator and steering the folk towards the new ministry.

When Stenhouse St Aidan's fell vacant again I felt I had been away long enough to be able to return and so filled in there for eighteen months. When I thought I had finished, St Colm's came along. Now here was a different ballgame! The congregation, very much my own age group with no young folk, knew they would not be allowed to call a minister and that they would be uniting with another congregation which turned out to be Gorgie Parish Church. So the sad demise of a congregation had to be coped with. I had to think out how to help them to cope with loss, which for some whose families had been long members was like bereavement, and at the same time encourage them to be open to what might lie ahead. It was a different kind of ministry for me. I think they would say I helped them through it.

Another retirement occupation has been chaplaincy to ministers and full-time workers in Presbytery. Edinburgh Presbytery has an organised scheme of pastoral care of such people. Six of us, mostly retired ministers ourselves, are allocated about fourteen clients to visit twice a year though in some cases there may be extra contact where there is illness, bereavement or other need. I find it a very pleasant occupation and those I have now been visiting for almost ten years have really become friends though on a professional basis.

Added to that I have had the great joy of marrying my own family and baptising grandchildren, and with the blessing of having all eleven grandchildren within easy reach, I have been closely involved in caring for some of them as they grew. The oldest is now at University herself.

*The whole family together, Christmas 2011*

## Chapter Eighteen: Reflections

I would not want to belong to any other denomination than the Church of Scotland. There is much to admire about several others and the Kirk can exasperate and annoy, but it has, even in this secular society, an access to people that is unrivalled, usually to those in need. I have met some great folk in ordinary congregations, truly the salt of the earth. The vast amount of voluntary work, often through community organisations, undertaken by its members without strings attached, is immeasurable. We give money and time and gifts with no requirement for response. What the Church does is hardly recognised and no credit given. We are there for people. Often of course there is response because when people allow themselves to listen and hear they recognise the truth, and God works and cannot be stopped whatever obstacles are put in the way.

As I have said, Scripture Union working in schools and the Scottish Bible Society both complement the work of the Church. But we must not allow ourselves to be silent in the face of opposition. Proclamation is our calling and we must be missionaries and have mission-orientated congregations.

It seems to me that nowhere in the Bible is the church seen as powerful. It was not envisaged as equalling the State but as leaven in the lump or the mustard seed and bringing the salt that increases savour. Though we have to proclaim, (because how will they hear without a preacher?) each hearer makes his/her own decision and gradually they come in. Our job is always to offer. Jesus did not find everyone flocking to him. There will always be those on the circumference and those at various points in between and those in the inner circle.

I cannot be a Scriptural literalist or how can I be a woman and a minister? Certainly the first person Jesus told to tell others that he was risen was a woman, Mary Magdalene. Of course explanations can be given for the words of Paul in the chaotic Corinthian setting and he himself said there were no differences, neither male nor female - "all are one in Christ Jesus" – and recognized the ministry of individual women in the churches he wrote to. I do also believe it is right to recognise a different era and a different culture. Conservatives in interpretation have also assumed the description evangelical. It is possible in fact to be evangelical but not conservative.

What I can never doubt along with those who struggled before me is my own call, nor can I deny that God has over and over again blessed my ministry for others and for myself. Those who have worked with me know that one of my favourite texts is *"Seek first the kingdom of God and all these things will be added to you as well."* I have proved that to be true. Through all the struggling and decision-making, the call of God did eventually come first, and I have had very great blessing. The family have done well, all graduates, a teacher, a minister, an architect, a freelance writer and researcher, and all are happily married, in two cases to partners they met through my moves, and have lovely children. I need not have feared for them.

In writing this as one, of whom there are not now many left, who can recall the days when the Church of Scotland did not allow a woman to fulfil her call, I want to pay tribute to those who broke down the barriers and so opened the way. Encouraging one another, as we are urged to do, is so important, and so I particularly want to draw attention to the men – *men* - who over the years gave me that constant encouragement. For these reasons I have told my story.

*With my youngest grandchild in November 2011*